FOOD MATTERS

EATING ORGANIC

by Rebecca Rissman

Content Consultant
Susan Oh, MS, MPH, RD, LD
Director, Research Nutrition Program
John Hopkins School of Medicine

Core Library
An Imprint of Abdo Publishing
abdopublishing.com

abdopublishing.com

Published by Abdo Publishing, a division of ABDO, PO Box 398166,
Minneapolis, Minnesota 55439. Copyright © 2016 by Abdo Consulting
Group, Inc. International copyrights reserved in all countries. No part of
this book may be reproduced in any form without written permission from
the publisher. Core Library™ is a trademark and logo of Abdo Publishing.

Printed in the United States of America, North Mankato, Minnesota
042015
092015

THIS BOOK CONTAINS
RECYCLED MATERIALS

Cover Photo: Lance Cheung/US Department of Agriculture
Interior Photos: Lance Cheung/US Department of Agriculture, 1, 10, 36,
45; US National Archives and Records Administration, 4; Greg Gibson/
AP Images, 7; Bob Nichols/US Department of Agriculture, 9, 34; David
Klobucar/KRT/Newscom, 12; Anson Eaglin/US Department of Agriculture,
14; Library of Congress, 16; iStockphoto, 21, 22, 40; Ingram Publishing/
Newscom, 24; Scott Bauer/US Department of Agriculture, 27; John
Eveson/FLPA ImageBroker/Newscom, 29; Custom Medical Stock Photo
"CMSP Biology"/Newscom, 31

Editor: Mirella Miller
Series Designer: Becky Daum

Library of Congress Control Number: 2015931586

Cataloging-in-Publication Data
Rissman, Rebecca.
 Eating organic / Rebecca Rissman.
   p. cm. -- (Food matters)
Includes bibliographical references and index.
ISBN 978-1-62403-862-4
1. Natural foods--Juvenile literature.   I. Title.
641.3/02--dc23
                                                    2015931586

CONTENTS

CHAPTER ONE

WHERE HAVE ALL THE BIRDS GONE?

n the 1960s, nature lovers noticed an upsetting trend. The songbirds in many areas of North America had fallen silent. After careful research, scientists learned the birds that had been singing cheerful morning songs were dying. Scientists were shocked when they learned nearby farms were causing the issue. But what was happening to kill all of these birds? And why?

Farmers sprayed pesticides such as DDT on their crops using airplanes for many years before realizing their harmful effects.

The farmers had not
meant to kill the birds.
They had sprayed their
crops with a synthetic
pesticide called DDT.
Synthetic pesticides are
man-made chemicals
used to kill insects or
other pests that harm
crops. DDT is especially
powerful. The birds were
eating insects that had
eaten the DDT-sprayed
crops. Then the birds
were dying.

After learning about
the effects of DDT and
other pesticides, many
people reconsidered
eating foods sprayed with

As scientists began to link human health to the health of the environment, eating organic became more popular.

the harmful chemicals. They chose to only eat foods grown without using man-made chemicals. These foods are called "organic." People believed eating organic would be healthier because they would be eating fewer foods with chemical residue. They also thought it would help the environment by reducing the amount of chemicals being sprayed.

Plant Growth

Organic plants are grown in a special way. These fruits, vegetables, and grains are grown without the use of synthetic pesticides, chemical fertilizers, or bioengineering. Chemical fertilizers are made up of inorganic material that has important nutrients for plant growth, but they often harm the soil and the surrounding ecosystem. They are added to fields to help plants grow. Chemical fertilizers must be added to the soil continually.

Bioengineering involves changing the genetic structure of a plant or animal in order to change the way it grows or behaves. Scientists can bioengineer plants and animals to grow faster, bigger, and heartier. This makes them more profitable when farmers sell them.

Organic farmers do not use any of these methods. They avoid synthetic pesticides, chemical fertilizers, and bioengineering. Organic farmers believe these methods can be harmful to the environment.

Organic farmers farm in ways that benefit
the environment.

Animals living on organic farms have space to roam and move around.

Livestock

Organic farmers use special methods to raise their livestock. The animals eat food labeled as organic. They have large living spaces with outdoor areas. Animals on non-organic farms often are raised in crowded and stressful areas. These conditions cause the animals to get sick often.

Organic livestock are not given antibiotics or growth hormones. Antibiotics are medicines that help animals recover from illness. They also can prevent the animals from getting sick. Growth hormones help the animals grow bigger. This means farmers produce more meat or milk. Organic farmers hope their animals grow using natural, non-chemical methods. They believe this is a better way to raise livestock.

Organic Labeling

Foods labeled as organic have met government standards for organic

Organic labels show shoppers an item was authorized organic by the US government.

foods. These guidelines differ slightly around the world. Organic foods generally are defined by how they are grown or raised.

In the United States, organic produce, meat, poultry, dairy, and eggs are marked with stickers, signs, or labels. The United States Department of Agriculture (USDA) certifies that foods are organic. Organic farms must do many things to earn their label. They must protect the environment, support animal welfare, avoid bioengineered products, and not use chemical fertilizers and synthetic pesticides. The USDA inspects organic farms each year to confirm they are following the guidelines.

Following the guidelines can be expensive and difficult. Many farmers must employ extra workers to keep their farms organic. They often have smaller harvests, which leads to organic foods being more expensive.

Many people choose to eat organic foods. Many Americans buy organic food at least some of the

In addition to produce, the USDA is responsible for inspecting meat, poultry, and some egg products in the United States.

time. This means organic farmers are very busy raising livestock and growing crops for hungry consumers. But is organic food actually healthier? And is it worth the higher price tag?

Biologist Rachel Carson published her book *Silent Spring* in 1962. The book discussed harmful effects pesticides had on nature. This excerpt shows the power of these chemicals:

> *Since the mid-1940s over 200 basic chemicals have been created for use in killing insects, weeds, rodents, and other organisms. . . .*
>
> *These sprays, dusts, and aerosols are now applied almost universally to farms, gardens, forests, and homes— nonselective chemicals that have the power to kill every insect, the "good" and the "bad," to still the song of birds and the leaping of fish in the streams, to coat the leaves with a deadly film, and to linger on in soil—all this though the intended target may be only a few weeds or insects.*

> Source: Rachel Carson. Silent Spring (Anniversary Edition).
> Boston: Houghton Mifflin, 2002. Print. 7.

Consider Your Audience

Read this excerpt from Carson's book carefully. If you were to rewrite this section for another audience, how would you change it? Imagine you are writing for a group of people who produce and sell pesticides, such as DDT. How is your tone different? Did you change any of the words? If so, explain why.

CHAPTER TWO

THE ROOTS OF ORGANIC FOOD

Until the late 1800s, some farming techniques resembled today's organic farming methods. Chemical fertilizers had not been invented yet. Pesticides were decades away from being used on farms. Farmers did not have access to bioengineering. They watched the seasons and carefully tended their soil.

Farmers in the 1800s and 1900s used small hand tools and animal labor to grow and harvest their crops.

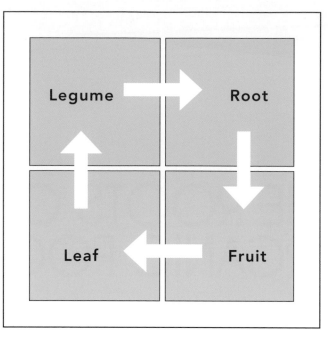

Crop Rotation

Farmers use crop rotation to keep their soil healthy. Different types of crops take different types of nutrients from the soil to grow. If only one type of crop is grown on a plot of land, all of one type of nutrient might be taken from the soil. After reading this chapter, why do you think rotating crops helps the soil?

Early farmers worked hard to keep their soil healthy. One way they did this was by rotating crops. Crop rotation involves planting different crops on a single plot of land over time. It often involves allowing the soil to "rest" with no crops for a season. For example, a farmer might plant corn on a plot of land one season, then soy the next. The farmer might let the soil rest the following season before beginning the pattern again. This prevents the soil from losing important nutrients and becoming unusable. Farmers have practiced crop rotation for centuries. In the early 1900s, crop rotation was a very important part of a farmer's job.

Pesticide Development

In the 1940s, the farming community changed with the discovery of the pesticide DDT. Many farmers began spraying their fields with other pesticides too. The pesticides quickly killed troublesome insects.

DDT's Unexpected Benefit

During World War II (1939–1945), US and British soldiers faced an outbreak of typhus. Lice and fleas spread this serious illness. These common pests were found in dirty and overcrowded war bunkers. Affected people were dusted with a powder containing DDT, which killed lice. Soon the epidemic was over. Scientists later used DDT to stop the spread of malaria. This deadly disease is passed on through mosquitoes. DDT is credited with saving millions of people from malaria.

Chemical fertilizers also became popular. They were an easy way to inject important nutrients into the soil.

The use of pesticides and fertilizers meant farmers could grow more crops with less manual labor. This was appealing to farmers who were spending long days working in the fields.

A small group of farmers continued to farm organically, however. They wanted to avoid chemical fertilizers and pesticides. They studied new information about farm ecosystems to grow their crops. This small group of farmers was unusual. Farmers who used chemical fertilizers and synthetic pesticides became the norm. In fact, they became known as conventional farmers.

Back to Nature

In the 1960s and 1970s, a social change happened in the United States. Young people called hippies focused on music, art, and doing things naturally. They embraced the idea of Mother Earth. They emphasized treating Earth well by not polluting. They pushed

Whole Foods Market was one of the first upscale grocery stores that carried organic foods.

turning "back to nature." This movement focused on the importance of organic farming methods.

By the 1990s and 2000s, organic farming became more common again. Organic foods were appealing to both farmers and shoppers. Fears about the effects of chemicals on foods and the environment led some shoppers to look for foods raised without them. They found organic foods at local markets, farm stands, and small produce stores. Some larger grocery store chains even began selling organic foods. Soon upscale

Some farmers use fertilizers on their fields to help with soil problems.

grocery stores that specialize in organic foods began appearing in big cities across the country. By 2003 shoppers could find organic foods in nearly 75 percent of the country's grocery stores.

Solving Problems

Some farmers turned to the organic movement as a solution to three common complaints. Many conventional farmers were struggling with bad soil from years of using chemical fertilizers. Without regularly rotating crops, their soil had lost nutrients and needed more and more chemical fertilizer. Second, farmers raising non-organic livestock were having trouble keeping their animals healthy. They were forced to give antibiotics to their livestock to keep them well. Farmers were paying for growth hormones too. These helped the livestock become big so they could produce more meat or milk. Third, fears about the effects of farming with synthetic pesticides, chemical fertilizers, bioengineering, antibiotics, and hormones threatened to hurt sales from conventional farms. People wanted to buy foods grown without the use of these methods. Farmers looking to solve all three of these problems turned to organic farming.

YOUR LIFE
Animal Rights

Many animal rights activists say organically raised livestock have a better quality of life than animals raised on conventional farms. This is because organic farms raise animals in larger, cleaner pens in order to keep them healthy. They are fed foods that are more similar to their natural diets. Conventional farms are often more crowded and dirty. They use antibiotics and hormones to keep their animals healthy. Do you think it matters how the animals are raised?

CHAPTER THREE

HOW ORGANIC FARMS WORK

Modern technology has made many tasks faster and easier for conventional farmers. How can organic farming compete? Organic farmers choose not to rely on the help of man-made chemicals. They must use a variety of alternative methods instead. Organic farmers focus on all parts of their farm ecosystem.

Some organic farmers use manure as fertilizer since it is natural.

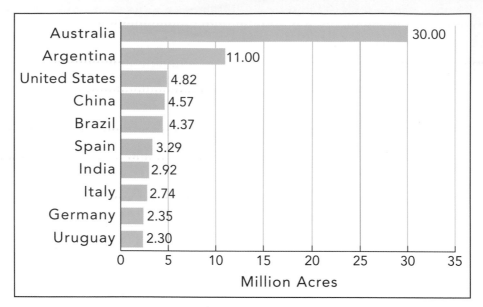

Organic Farmland

This simple chart shows where the most organic farmland is found around the world. Are you surprised to see the United States does not have the most organic farmland?

Soil and Weeds

The most important part of the farm ecosystem is the soil. Organic farmers use natural fertilizers, such as manure or compost. Manure is the waste that comes from farm animals, such as cows. Compost is a mixture of broken-down natural elements, such as rotting wood, food, and plants. Manure and compost keep farmers' soil moist, rich, and full of nutrients.

Organic farmers use alternative methods for weeding their crops. Also, they do not use fertilizers made with chemical ingredients.

Organic farmers deal with weeds in ways that are not harmful to the soil. They do not spray chemical weed killers. Organic farmers use crop rotation to reduce the number of weeds that grow around their crops. They use methods such as weed burning to keep their fields weed free. Farmers who burn their weeds use tools such as flamethrowers to light weeds on fire. They must be very careful to keep the fire from harming their food crops or spreading.

The freedom to move, as well as the exposure to fresh air, helps keep organic animals strong and healthy.

Pests and Animals

Pests are a problem for both conventional farms and organic farms. Organic farms use non-chemical methods for pest control. One method is to use trap crops. These are special plants that attract pests. Farmers plant trap crops near their food crops. Trap crops draw pests away from the valuable product. Organic farmers also use pest traps. These devices capture and kill the pests before they can harm crops.

All livestock farmers work hard to keep their animals healthy. Organic farmers do not give their animals antibiotics. This means they must use other methods to prevent illness. One method is keeping the animals in big, clean spaces. The farmers also use special feeding methods instead of hormones to help the animals grow big and strong. Many organic farmers allow their animals

Farmers' Use of Bioengineering

Bioengineering is a technology that allows scientists to influence the genes of living beings. It can be used to make a plant resistant to pests or grow extra quickly. For these reasons, bioengineered species are very appealing to farmers. Durable, fast-growing crops are easier to farm and can allow a farmer to make more money. Conventional farms use bioengineering in different ways. Some farmers grow bioengineered crops. Others feed their livestock bioengineered plants. Organic farms do not use any bioengineered products at all.

One bioengineered grass seed grows slower, which means it requires less mowing and watering.

to graze in fields. This is similar to the animals' natural feeding habits.

Bioengineering

Bioengineering is a new science. It involves changing the genes of a living thing. Organic farmers do not use any bioengineered seed or feed. They believe these products can change the ecosystem in a harmful way. Conventional farmers often rely on bioengineering. Some farmers plant bioengineered seeds for their crops. Others feed their livestock food made from bioengineered plants.

Differences

One of the most noticeable differences between the products from an organic farm and a conventional farm is the way they look. Organic crops are often smaller. Organic animals are also often smaller than conventionally raised livestock. Organic farmers are okay with this. They believe imperfect appearances do not affect the taste or quality of their product.

FURTHER EVIDENCE

Chapter Three discusses how organic farms work. What was one of the chapter's main points? What are some pieces of evidence in the chapter that support this main point? Check out the website at the link below. Does the information on this website support one of the main points in this chapter? Write a few sentences using new information from the website as evidence to support one of the main points in this chapter.

Learn about Organic Farms

mycorelibrary.com/eating-organic

Mark Lynas is an environmentalist and author. This excerpt is from a speech he gave about the organic food movement:

> If you think about it, the organic movement is at its heart a rejectionist one. It doesn't accept many modern technologies on principle. Like the Amish . . . who froze their technology with the horse and cart in 1850, the organic movement essentially freezes its technology in somewhere around 1950, and for no better reason. . . .
>
> In reality there is no reason at all why avoiding chemicals should be better for the environment – quite the opposite in fact. Recent research by Jesse Ausubel and colleagues at Rockefeller University looked at how much extra farmland Indian farmers would have had to cultivate today using the technologies of 1961 to get today's overall yield. The answer is 65 million hectares, an area the size of France.

Source: Mark Lynas. "Lecture to Oxford Farming Conference, 3 January 2013." Mark Lynas. Mark Lynas, January 3, 2013. Web. Accessed. January 26, 2015.

What's the Big Idea?

Read this excerpt closely. What point is Lynas trying to make about organic farming? Pick out two details that support this point. Does Lynas's tone impact the way you read this text?

CHAPTER FOUR

THE PROS AND CONS OF EATING ORGANIC

Organic farmers go to a great deal of trouble to grow foods without the use of chemicals. But does it matter? Are organic foods healthier? Are fertilizers, pesticides, and bioengineered products harmful? What are the pros and cons of eating organic food?

Organic farmers work hard to grow foods that are healthy and safe for consumers to buy and eat.

Healthy soil is important for farms to be successful.

All About Organic

There are many pros to eating organic. One common argument for organic farming is that it is good for the environment. Because organic farmers do not use artificial pesticides and fertilizers, these chemicals do not leak into the farms' surroundings. And because farmers do not need large machinery to spread these chemicals, organic farms often use much less energy than conventional farms. This means organic farms pollute less than conventional farms.

The importance of healthy soil in organic farming also is very helpful to the environment. Organic farmers can use the same land for a long time. Some conventional farming methods exhaust the soil. Sometimes conventional farmers are forced to abandon their fields. Doing so wastes energy, resources, and land because farmers are forced to start over in a new area.

Organic farms help the environment by supporting biodiversity. This means they help a variety of living beings to grow. Conventional farms use pesticides that often kill more than just the intended pests. They kill other living beings that are accidentally exposed to the pesticides. This can

Using Manure

Conventional and organic farms use manure to fertilize their fields. Organic farms often buy manure from other organic farms. Or they get it from their own livestock. In small quantities, manure is a very helpful farming tool. Conventional livestock farms often produce huge quantities of manure. Sometimes they make so much they are forced to store it in pits. Spills or leaks from the manure pits can be very harmful. They can lead to water or air pollution, as well as serious illnesses for both humans and animals.

affect entire food chains and hurt animals that are not pests. Practicing organic pest control helps protect a variety of living beings in the farms' surroundings.

Animal rights activists often point out another pro of organic farming. They believe animals raised on organic farms have a better quality of life. They point to the diet, lifestyle, and larger size of animal spaces as proof of this.

Buying Non-Organic

There are cons to eating organic. The biggest con for most consumers is the high price of organic products. Organic foods cost 20 to 100 percent more than non-organic foods. This is because organic farmers must spend more time laboring over their crops. The higher price tag makes it hard for some people to afford and eat organic foods. It also makes organic farming unrealistic for poor and developing nations that need to produce food more cheaply.

Another con is that organic farms typically produce less food than conventional farms. They also cannot grow crops out of season. This means summer plants, such as tomatoes and berries, cannot be grown on organic farms located in places that have harsh winters. Consumers who are looking to buy these foods must either buy conventional tomatoes and berries or none at all. This is a con for people who want to buy the foods they like year round.

Many people wonder if organic foods are healthier than non-organic foods. This is a complicated issue. Some conventionally farmed foods contain traces of the chemicals used to farm

YOUR LIFE
Learning to Read Labels

How can you tell if your produce is from an organic farm or a conventional farm? Read the label. Most produce sold in grocery stores is tagged with small stickers showing the Produce Lookup (PLU) code. The first digit in each PLU will tell you how the produce was grown. A PLU starting with 9 means the product was grown organically. And a four-digit PLU starting with 3 or 4 usually means the product was grown conventionally.

It is important to eat a variety of foods that will help your body to grow strong and healthy.

them. There may also be antibiotics in the animal's meat. Some people worry the foods could be harmful when eaten. Supporters of organic foods feel these chemicals should be avoided whenever possible.

There is not much evidence to prove or disprove non-organic foods are harmful. Many of the chemicals, bioengineered products, hormones, and antibiotics used in conventional farming are very new. Scientists have not had time to test their long-term effects on humans. People who prefer to eat conventionally grown foods consider this to be a con for organic foods. They feel as though there is not enough clear data to support the idea that organic foods are better.

Ultimately every individual needs to choose whether or not to eat organic foods. Some people eat only organic foods. Others choose to eat some organic foods. Many people eat no organic foods at all. Learning more about this issue, including the way conventional farms may affect human health and the environment, can help you to make the decision for yourself.

EXPLORE ONLINE

The focus in Chapter Four is on the pros and cons of eating organic. The website below also focuses on making the decision to eat organic or not. As you know, every source is different. How is the information on the website different from the information in this chapter? What information is the same? How do the two sources present information differently? What can you learn from this website?

Is Eating Organic Better?

mycorelibrary.com/eating-organic

- Organic plants are grown without the use of synthetic pesticides, chemical fertilizers, or bioengineering. Organic livestock are raised without antibiotics or growth hormones.

- Pesticides and chemical fertilizers are man-made chemicals farmers use to kill pests and inject nutrients into the soil.

- Bioengineering is a type of science that involves changing the genes of living beings. Bioengineered crops can be designed to resist pesticides or grow very large.

- Growth hormones are man-made chemicals farmers use to make their livestock grow bigger or produce more milk.

- Antibiotics are medicines fed to livestock to help prevent common illnesses.

- If you are at a grocery store, check the PLU label on the produce. If the number starts with a 9, it was grown organically.

- Eating organic is better for the environment and for the treatment of animals.

IN THE KITCHEN

Organic Black Bean and Avocado Salsa

15 oz. can organic black beans, drained and rinsed

11 oz. can organic whole kernel sweet corn, drained

4 organic tomatoes

1/2 organic bell pepper

1/4 organic red onion

1 organic avocado

1/2 bunch fresh, organic cilantro

2 organic limes

2 tablespoons red wine vinegar

1 teaspoon salt

1/2 teaspoon pepper

Ask an adult to help you with this recipe.
Chop vegetables into small cubes and mix together in a
large bowl. Roughly chop the cilantro and add it to the bowl.
Juice the two limes into the mixture, then add the vinegar,
salt, and pepper. Stir well and refrigerate. Serve with organic
tortilla chips and enjoy!

Surprise Me

This book talks about the importance of soil in organic farming. Organic farmers spend a great deal of time making sure their soil is in good condition. After reading this book, what two or three facts about soil did you find most surprising? Write a few sentences about each fact. Why did you find them surprising?

Take a Stand

This book discusses eating only organic foods. Many people claim it is healthier and better for the environment. What do you think? Do you think it is best to eat only organic foods? Write a short essay explaining your opinion. Remember to give reasons for your opinion, with details and facts supporting your argument.

Say What?

Discussing organic eating involves learning many new vocabulary words. Find five words in this book you had never heard before. Use a dictionary to find out what they mean. Then write the meanings in your own words and use each word in a new sentence.

You Are There

This book talks about how organic farmers grow crops. Imagine you are working on an organic farm. Write a diary entry about a day of farm work, including weeding, pest control, and caring for the animals. Include as many details about your day as you can.

GLOSSARY

animal rights
the idea that animals should not be used in medical testing, hunted, or treated unkindly

biodiversity
the variety of life forms found in an ecosystem

compost
broken-down matter used to keep soil healthy

conventional farms
farms that use chemical fertilizers, pesticides, and bioengineering

ecosystem
all the living beings interacting in a biological community

food chain
a series of living beings in which each depends upon the next as a food source

growth hormones
chemicals that stimulate growth

manual labor
work done without the help of machinery

synthetic pesticide
a poisonous chemical made to resist and kill pests

LEARN MORE

Books

Friedman, Lauri S. Ed. *Organic Food and Farming.* Detroit: Greenhaven Press, 2010.

Pollan, Michael. *The Omnivore's Dilemma: The Secrets Behind What You Eat.* New York: Dial Books, 2009.

Vogel, Julia. *Save the Planet: Local Farms and Sustainable Foods.* Ann Arbor, MI: Cherry Lake, 2010.

Websites

To learn more about Food Matters, visit **booklinks.abdopublishing.com**. These links are routinely monitored and updated to provide the most current information available.

Visit **mycorelibrary.com** for free additional tools for teachers and students.

INDEX

ABOUT THE AUTHOR

Rebecca Rissman is an award-winning children's author and editor. She has written more than 200 books about history, culture, science, and art. She lives in Portland, Oregon, with her husband and daughter.